GUIDELINES
FOR TESTING
Psychic
CLAIMANTS

GUIDELINES

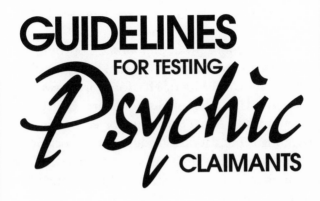

FOR TESTING

Psychic

CLAIMANTS

RICHARD WISEMAN, PH.D.
UNIVERSITY OF HERTFORDSHIRE

ROBERT L. MORRIS, PH.D.
EDINBURGH UNIVERSITY

Prometheus Books

59 John Glenn Drive
Amherst, NewYork 14228-2197

Published 1995 by Prometheus Books

99 98 97 96 95   5 4 3 2 1

Library of Congress Cataloging-in-Publication Data

Wiseman, Richard (Richard John), 1966–
    Guidelines for testing psychic claimants / Richard Wiseman, Robert L. Morris.
        p.   cm.
    Includes bibliographical references.
    ISBN 1–57392–028–2 (alk. paper)
    1. Psychic ability—Testing. 2. Fraud. I. Morris, Robert L. (Robert Lyle), 1942–   . II. Title.
BF1031.W735   1995
133.8'028'7—dc20   95–31632
                                                            CIP

Printed in the United States of America on acid-free paper

To Rex Cooper

Contents

Acknowledgments

This book could not have been produced without the advice, help and assistance of many people. First and foremost, our thanks go to the John Björkhem Memorial Foundation for funding the entire project. Thanks also to John Beloff, Tony Cornell, Deborah Delanoy, Hilary Evans, Julie Milton, Tom Ruffles, Matthew Smith, Robin Taylor, and Donald West for their constructive comments on earlier drafts of these guidelines. Ours thanks to Charles Cameron, Daryl Bem, David Berglas, George Hansen, Erlendur Haraldsson, David Marks, Max Maven, and Marcello Truzzi for their constructive comments on the issues discussed in this publication. We are also grateful to Katie Moore for providing support during the project's initial stages. Special thanks to the Mary Evans Picture Library and University of London for kindly providing the illustrations. Finally, thanks to Bill Forster who, on behalf of

University of Hertfordshire, took on the publishing of the book and whose guidance has been invaluable.

Introduction

Parapsychology has been defined as the study of apparent new means of communication between people and their environment. Most parapsychologists draw a distinction between two types of ostensible psychic ability. In extra-sensory perception (ESP), information appears to flow from the environment to a person, using a channel of communication not presently understood. For example, an alleged psychic may apparently divine the contents of a sealed envelope, or accurately predict a future event. In the second type of psychic ability, psychokinesis (PK), a person appears to influence the environment using unknown means. For example, an alleged psychic may apparently cause a table to levitate by concentrating on it, or bend a spoon by gently rubbing it.

Generally speaking, there are two ways in which para-psychologists investigate the possible existence of psychic ability. Some researchers assume that everybody possesses such abilities to a small degree. These researchers carry out experiments on large numbers of individuals, none of whom claim to be especially psychic. The effects obtained in these studies are often small and can only be detected by statistical analysis. An alternative approach concentrates on "psychic claimants," that is, individuals who *do* claim to be psychically gifted. Studies employing this latter approach typically employ just one subject (the claimant in question) and when successful, produce effects so large (such as the levitation of a table) that they can be observed without the aid of statistics. Both approaches have yielded interesting and useful data. Edge, Morris, Palmer, and Rush (1986) give an excellent overview of the methods and results obtained from "multi-subject" studies. Similarly, Beloff (1993) gives an admirable historical review of single subject investigations. However, even a casual observer of this literature couldn't fail to notice that this latter approach has only been adopted by a minority of researchers. This bias is unfortunate, as the study of psychic claimants could prove important for several reasons. For example, Braude (1986) has argued that, like many other human abilities, such as creativity, psychic ability might best be studied *in extremis,* rather than as it occurs in the "normal" population. In addition, the phenomena produced by such claimants are to many (including, perhaps, most of the general public), more convincing evidence of psychic ability than the statistical data from "multi-subject" studies.

Researchers have avoided working with psychic

claimants in part because there have existed no formal methodological guidelines as to how such work should proceed. This manual tackles this problem by providing pragmatic and flexible guidelines to help researchers identify and resolve the problems that most frequently occur during the assessment of individuals claiming strong psychic ability.

1

The Problem of Fraud

Psychic fraud . . . has been the single most important factor in damaging the reputation of parapsychology and retarding its growth."

John Palmer (1988, p. 109)

Many psychic claimants have been the subject of scientific scrutiny. Around the turn of the century psychical researchers investigated well-known mediums such as Daniel Home and Eusapia Palladino. More recently parapsychologists have examined individuals such as Ted Serios, Bill Delmore, and Uri Geller.

Unfortunately, some claimants have proved to be "pseudo-psychics," that is individuals who consciously fake psychic ability. For example, in 1906 the *Journal of the Society for Psychical Research* published an exposure of a medium named Charles Eldred. At the start of his séances, Eldred sat in a large chair in a curtained off area of the room (called a "séance cabinet"). The lights were lowered and various spirits would apparently materialize within this "cabinet" and move around the séance room. It was eventually discovered that the back of Eldred's chair housed a secret compartment which, when forced open, contained the masks, cloth, beards, and wigs that Eldred used to fake spirit entities. More recently, Delaney (1987) has described how researchers at Edinburgh University were approached by a seventeen-year-old boy claiming genuine PK ability. This claimant performed many informal demonstrations of his apparent psychic metal-bending and fire-raising abilities. The investigators became suspicious and secretly filmed the claimant during testing. The film revealed undeniable proof of trickery and, when confronted with this evidence, the claimant admitted that all his demonstrations had been fraudulent. These examples are not isolated instances of cheating. Such trickery has continually dogged parapsychology (see, for example, Kurtz 1985; Hansen 1990).

Failure to detect such fraud can lead to serious negative consequences. For example, in Project Alpha (see Randi 1983a, 1983b; Truzzi 1987) two known pseudopsychics were sent by magician James Randi to be assessed at the McDonnell Parapsychology Laboratory. Although researchers at the laboratory did not make any formal statements as to the validity of the claimants' psychic ability, neither did they manage to detect the trickery used by the two men. Randi's revelation of the hoax contributed to the loss of funding, and eventual closure, of the McDonnell Laboratory. Failure to discover subject cheating can also result in widespread negative publicity. Project Alpha was reported in *Discover* magazine, the *Washington Post,* and the *New York Times.* The controversy that surrounds the possible fraudulent nature of claimants can also threaten the unity of parapsychology. Arguments concerning the validity of the claims of medium Mina Crandon almost split apart the American Society for Psychical Research (Tietze 1973).

Researchers who fail to guard against such cheating also face the problem of false accusations. This problem can perhaps best be illustrated with a hypothetical example. Let us imagine that an individual with genuine psychic ability approaches researchers and wishes to be tested. Both researchers and claimant may invest considerable time and money in the design and running of pilot studies and formal experimentation. Further, let us imagine that the claimant produces genuine psychic phenomena. If the researchers have not correctly designed, run, and reported this experiment, critics may be able to explain away their results as possibly being due to fraud. If this is the case, the efforts of researchers and claimant will have been wasted. In addition, the claimant may have to face the unpleasant experience of being labeled a cheat and this, in turn, may dissuade other claimants from becoming involved in parapsychological testing.

2

Initial Meetings with the Claimant

Before embarking on any type of experimentation, researchers should try to build up a general picture of the
claimant and of the claims being made including, for
example, the reasons behind the claimant's wish to be
tested, and an exact description of the ability that is being
claimed. Any ethical problems that might arise should also
be identified at this point. These aims can be achieved in
one or two well thought out meetings with the claimant.
This section discusses some of the questions that researchers might find it helpful to address during these
meetings.

In What Context Does the Individual Use the Claimed Abilities?

Psychic claimants use their alleged abilities in a variety of
settings. Some act as counselors, helping others to identify

and solve personal problems. Palmists, astrologers, and readers of tarot cards or crystal balls usually fall into this category. Mediums can act as a rather unusual type of bereavement counselor, claiming to help individuals communicate with their deceased friends and relatives. Others, such as faith healers and psychic surgeons, obviously work within a medical context. Psychic detectives work in a forensic setting, offering advice to law enforcement agencies in the hope of preventing, or solving, a crime. Other claimants operate in religious settings, using their alleged ability to help attract followers to their particular religious organization or maintain their loyalty. Alleged psychics are also used within industrial and business settings. These individuals often work as consultants, being asked, for example, to psychically divine productive sites for mineral extraction, advise on personnel selection, or psychically predict the future of financial markets. Finally, many claimants do not use their apparent abilities for any particular purpose. These individuals may believe that they can do something rather unusual but cannot see any use for their ability, or are unwilling to apply it in a practical way.

What is the Claimant's Motivation for Being Investigated?

Claimants can have a whole host of possible motives for being involved in testing. Some are unsure whether their abilities are genuine or the result of self-deception, and approach investigators to obtain an expert opinion. Others may be genuinely convinced that they are psychic, but need an expert to validate this belief. For example, a faith healer or psychic counselor may be able to attract more clients if he or she can display evidence of having been investigated, and validated, by scientists. Alternatively, a claimant may not want to be psychic, but may have had several unusual experiences (e.g., dreams coming true, thinking of somebody a short time before they telephone) and may wish to undergo testing to prove that these experiences were not due to psychic ability. Another possibility is that the claimant is intending to deceive the investigator and is therefore motivated by the rewards derived from such trickery. It is important that researchers understand the diverse range of factors that motivate the pseudopsychic. Some may be motivated by financial reward. Such payment may come directly from researchers who offer claimants large amounts of money to undergo testing. Alternatively, these payments may come from the boost to business that a pseudopsychic receives after researchers have erroneously validated his or her ability. Pseudopsychics may also enjoy the increased attention they will receive from their friends, relatives, researchers, and the media as a result of being investigated. In addition, pseudopsychics may be motivated by the increased personal power they expect to receive from being validated by scientists. Finally, researchers should be aware that some pseudopsychics have, in the past, been motivated by little more than the increase in self-esteem that comes through fooling scientists.

What Is the Claimant's Background?

Researchers will of course discover information concerning the claimant's background during the course of initial meetings. However, it is especially important that researchers try to assess whether the claimant has the ability to successfully cheat during testing. Researchers could, for example, try to assess the claimant's level of knowledge concerning conjuring and psychic fraud. There is obviously no easy way to assess this issue; a claimant who is intending to cheat is unlikely to admit to having this type of information. For example, "Tim," the pseudopsychic investigated by Delanoy (1987), was a member of the International Brotherhood of Magicians (IBM), but he only admitted to this fact after being caught cheating. However, researchers can check the membership lists of these organizations at a local, national, and international level (see Appendix B). In addition, researchers could attempt to discover whether the claimant has any informal contacts with the magical or pseudopsychic communities. This is perhaps best achieved by researchers joining (or at least forming friendly links with) these organizations themselves.

Researchers should also attempt to discover whether the claimant has been caught cheating, or has been accused of cheating during previous testing. Again, the pseudopsychic may attempt to conceal such information. Hansen (1990) describes how Steve Shaw (one of the pseudopsychics involved in Project Alpha) had been accused of trickery prior to Project Alpha, yet did not mention this to investigators at the McDonnell Laboratory. As before, researchers need to carry out some simple detective work. This could include undertaking a literature search for any articles that mention previous testing of the claimant. In addition, investigators should establish informal contact with other researchers who carry out this type of work, thus increasing the chances of discovering evidence of fraud that has not been committed to print.

What Type of Psychic Ability Is Being Claimed?

The introduction discussed how most parapsychologists draw a distinction between two types of psychic ability, namely, ESP and PK. Further distinctions are made within these categories. Claims for ESP are commonly grouped into three subdivisions. The term "telepathy" (also referred to as "general ESP" or "GESP") is used to refer to situations in which an individual appears to access, by unknown means, information known to one or more other people. For example, a deck of playing cards may be shuffled and then each card looked at by a "sender" who attempts to psychically broadcast this information to a "receiver." Clairvoyance refers to situations in which an individual appears to access information not known to others. For example, in the experiment outlined above, the claimant would try to divine the order of the shuffled deck *before* anybody looks at the faces of the cards. Finally, precognition refers to situations in which an individual appears to access information concerning a future event. Here the claimant would attempt to predict the order of the playing cards before they were shuffled; after the shuffling the predicted order would be compared with the actual order.

Claims for PK are commonly grouped into two subdivisions. First, "micro-PK" occurs when a claimant appears to psychically bias the behavior of a physical system that normally behaves in a random way, such as the roll of a fair die or a random number generator (RNG). Second, "macro-PK" occurs when a claimant apparently uses psychic ability to alter the properties of a physical object, or of a stable system (e.g., the temperature of a room). Many individuals have attempted to classify the range of macro-PK abilities that could, theoretically, be possessed by a claimant (possibly the most thorough analysis is that presented by Fitzkee 1944). The following six categories appear to have some heuristic value. First, "appearances"' consist of the production of an object as, for example, when Sai Baba (a well-known Indian religious leader) apparently produces gold trinkets within his empty hands. The second category, "vanishes," entails the claimant apparently making an object disappear (the opposite of "appearances"). The third category, "transportations" (or "teleportations") is essentially a combination of the first two categories, involving the disappearance of an object from one location, and its subsequent reappearance at another location. The fourth category is that of "penetrations." This occurs when an object appears to penetrate some form of barrier, without either the object or barrier being damaged. The barrier itself may be a physical object or biological system. For example, a faith healer may appear to penetrate a patient's skin without it showing any signs of incision. A fifth category is that of "modifications," which occur when an object undergoes apparent transformation in type, property, form, size, or color. For example, the famous medium, D. D. Home, was reportedly able to modify himself, such that he was able to pick up hot coals in his bare hands, without harm. Finally, the sixth category consists of the application of force. This category includes several diverse phenomena, such as the apparent levitation of an object, the adherence of the target object to another object, and the animation of the target. The vast range of "telekinetic" effects apparently displayed by many physical mediums would fall into this category.

Does the Claimant Believe that Certain Conditions Are Conducive to His or Her Psychic Ability?

A claimant may state that his or her psychic ability only manifests itself under certain conditions, and/or cannot function under others. These conditions usually fall into one of three categories. First, some claimants say that they need to perform under certain physical conditions. For example, a medium may demand that no white light is allowed in the séance room, or that a certain section of that room is partitioned off to form a "spirit cabinet." Second, claimants may require certain observational conditions. A claimant may say that they cannot demonstrate macro-PK while being directly observed, or in front of skeptical individuals. Finally, claimants may state that they themselves need to be in some type of psychological condition, such as some form of altered state of consciousness.

A Short List of Questions

The above sections have discussed the background to some of the more important issues that should be discussed during initial meetings with the claimant. To further aid this process, researchers may find it helpful to ask (either formally or informally) the following questions[1]:

1. Could you please describe your apparent psychic ability?
2. What sorts of events initially led you to believe that you possess this ability?
3. Could you please describe one or two instances in which your ability appeared especially striking or impressive?
4. Have you looked for any normal explanations for these events (i.e., what makes you believe that they might be paranormal)?
5. Have you noticed any factors that systematically affect your ability (e.g., when it occurs, the psychological state that you are in, what type of objects seem to be affected, who else is around, etc.)?

---

1. These questions are loosely based upon material in Appendix A in Auerbach (1986).

6. Do you have a theory as to what might be going on?

7. Did you have an interest in apparent psychic phenomena before these events?

8. Have you contacted any "experts" before now (e.g., the police, psychologists, parapsychologists, priests)? If so, what has been their reaction?

9. Have you read any books or articles about supposed psychic phenomena? If so, which ones?

10. Are you a member of any organization connected with supposed psychic phenomena (e.g., the Society for Psychical Research, the American Society for Psychical Research)?

11. Are you a member of any organization connected with stage magic and conjuring (e.g., the International Brotherhood of Magicians)?

12. Have you received any publicity or media attention regarding your apparent ability?

13. Could you please briefly outline the factors and events that led you to this organization?

Developing a Testable Claim

Before attempting any experimentation it is vital that researchers have a thorough understanding of the individual's claim. This includes understanding the nature of, for example, the claimed ability, the type of target material the claimant likes to work with, and the conditions under which this ability apparently manifests itself.

Some claimants may approach researchers with a very

vague, ill-defined, claim. For example, the claimant may state that he or she can demonstrate some form of macro-PK, but that this ability is unpredictable, so that he or she is unsure exactly when phenomena will occur or what they will be. If this is the case, researchers should realize that they could be dealing with one of two possible scenarios. First, the claimant may be being quite honest and simply may not know the nature of her/his abilities, or is unable to express them in greater detail. Second, the claimant may be a pseudopsychic who consciously avoids making a specific claim to help deceive researchers. This latter stratagem is frequently used by pseudopsychics and serves two purposes. First, it is very difficult to adequately prepare to test a claim, or observe a demonstration, without first knowing what phenomena are likely to occur. Second, this stratagem also helps the trickster should a demonstration not go according to plan. As noted by Robert-Houdin (1877, p. 33):

> However skilful the performer may be, and however complete his preparations for a given trick, it is still possible that some unforeseen accident may cause a failure. The only way to get out of such a difficulty is to finish the trick in another manner. But to be able to do this, the performer must have strictly complied with this important rule: *never announce beforehand the nature of the effect that you intend to produce* [emphasis ours].

For this reason, researchers should ensure that a detailed claim is specified before any experimentation. If a claimant appears unsure as to the factors that are conducive to his or her ability, researchers should help identify such factors. This could involve running several informal sessions (i.e., with no or few controls present) in which the claimant can attempt to produce phenomena under a variety of circumstances. Before undertaking such sessions, researchers should clearly inform the claimant that any phenomena produced will not be taken as evidence of psychic ability. This may help avoid a claimant erroneously believing (and perhaps telling others) that he or she has been formally "tested" when, in reality, only pilot investigations have taken place.

Ethical Concerns

There are many ethical problems that could arise from testing. For example, the claimant may derive a feeling of psychological well-being (e.g., increased self-esteem) through believing that he or she is psychic. Negative test results may destroy this feeling and could lead to a variety of harmful consequences (e.g., depression or feeling worthless). Second, the opposite situation, although perhaps less likely, could prove equally as harmful. A claimant may not want to be psychic, but may have had several unusual, and worrying, experiences. Positive test results in this latter situation could prove as harmful as negative ones in the former. In addition, other individuals may have placed considerable faith in the notion that the claimant is psychic. Negative test results could leave such individuals with severe problems. For example, a recently bereaved widow in need of counselling may devote herself (both financially and emotionally) to a fake medium. Such an individual may feel lost, confused, and angry if an investigation reveals that this medium was not psychic, or (worse still) was fraudulent. Finally, a claimant may be suffering from some kind of delusional belief system or from paranoia. Interacting with researchers may be viewed by such an individual as verification of their beliefs, and thus help reinforce and elaborate these systems of thought.

There is no straightforward advice that can be given here. As with all research involving human participants, investigators should be familiar with standard texts on research ethics (see Appendix A), such that they can responsibly assess the effects that testing might have on claimants and those around them. In addition, researchers should be sensitive to the fact that, on occasion, a claimant may benefit more from interacting with a clinical psychologist and/or psychiatrist than having his or her paranormal claims evaluated. For this reason researchers may find it helpful to form contacts with local mental health practitioners, and, when necessary, be prepared to liaise with them during an investigation.

3

Working with Likely Tricksters

After a few meetings with the claimant, researchers have to decide whether they wish to embark on an investigation. Researchers may consider such work unfeasible or undesirable. A claimant may not be able to formulate a claim that can easily be tested. Alternatively, the claimant may appear mentally unstable or physically threatening. However, one factor that should be given serious attention is the degree to which researchers believe the claimant is likely to be a pseudopsychic. Their judgment will depend on several factors including, for example, evidence or accusations of cheating in past studies; the claimant's level of knowledge about trickery; the claimant having suspicious motives for wanting to be tested; and even the researchers' intuitive feelings. Problems arise if the researchers suspect that the claimant might be a likely trickster. This section discusses some of the issues involved in working with such an individual.

Advantages and Disadvantages of Working with Likely Tricksters

There are several disadvantages associated with attempting to assess claimants who seem likely to engage in trickery. First, there is an increased likelihood of being the target of subject deception. If such cheating goes undetected, researchers could face many of the negative consequences outlined in chapter 1. Second, some skeptics (e.g., Kurtz 1985) have argued that if a claimant has been caught cheating in the past, all data from that claimant should be dismissed as worthless. If researchers, or their anticipated readership, are convinced by this argument, they may see little point in working with individuals who have already been exposed as tricksters. Third, researchers may believe that such work endorses psychic fraud and agree with Eleanor Sidgwick (1909) when she wrote that,

A method from the turn of the century for faking a levitation in a darkened séance room. *Mary Evans Picture Library*

A "materialized" hand being faked in a slightly different way. *Mary Evans Picture Library*

> so long as the fees of investigators . . . flow with
> unabated abundance into the pockets of mediums who
> have been detected in deliberate trickery, this trickery
> will also remain unabated. (p. 307)

However, some writers have argued that there are a number of advantages associated with assessing such subjects. First, as noted by Beloff (1991), refusal to work with a high-risk subject may result in missing the opportunity to obtain, and record, genuine psychic phenomena. Beloff illustrates his argument with the career of Eusapia Palladino. Beloff first describes how Palladino was often caught cheating in many of her séances, held around the turn of this century. He then goes on to note that he regards a set of séances as having resulted in the production of genuine phenomena. Beloff argues that these "genuine" phenomena would have been missed had the investigators adhered to the "once a cheat. always a cheat" hypothesis, and thus refused to work with Palladino. Second, Beloff (1984) has also noted that researchers should perhaps seek out high-risk subjects, given that some theoreticians (e.g., Batcheldor 1966) have suggested that a certain amount of trickery may be needed to act as a catalyst for genuine psychic phenomena.

Again, little advice can be given here. Researchers must decide for themselves whether the advantages of working with a high-risk claimant outweigh the disadvantages.

Level of Experimental Security Needed When Working with Likely Tricksters

If researchers do decide to work with likely tricksters, it is vital that maximum safeguards are enforced to counter potential fraud. However, when investigating claimants who appear completely honest, researchers may be tempted to employ few safeguards against trickery. Such temptation should be resisted, and researchers should design and run their investigation assuming cheating *will* be attempted. As noted by Collins (1983),

> a subject with a completely innocent history must be treated, as far as experimental design is concerned, in the same way as the most notorious cheat. (p. 929)

Researchers may feel awkward implementing counter-deception measures against claimants who appear totally honest. If this is the case, researchers should remind themselves of the following points. First, competent pseudopsychics have often faked honesty, sincerity, and friendliness. For example, Delanoy (1987) has described how one pseudopsychic employed consummate acting skills in an attempt to convince his investigators that his abilities were genuine. Delanoy notes:

> I felt I had come to know Tim [the pseudopsychic] fairly well. We had established what appeared to be an honest, friendly and trusting rapport. . . . [Tim] devoted a great deal of his time to working with us, and also had a relatively long journey getting to and from our lab. These things, particularly when combined with his very co-operative and friendly manner may well have biased me towards liking him. This in turn may have colored my perspective in viewing his claims. (pp. 252–55)

Second, researchers should remind themselves that a poorly designed study of an honest claimant (i.e., an individual who does not intend to deceive researchers) is likely to be criticized unless it contains suitable controls against fraud. Controls exist, in part, to help protect such individuals from unfair criticism that might emerge after the completion of a study.

4

General Research Policies

For research to happen, both claimant and researcher need to decide that they wish to work with one another. The previous section discussed issues surrounding whether researchers wished to work with a claimant. This section concentrates on whether the claimant will wish to work with researchers. This decision often revolves around whether the general aims and methods of research are acceptable to the claimant. To help prevent potential misunderstanding about these points, researchers may find it helpful to outline these topics in a short document that could be circulated to potential claimants. This document should be designed to discourage pseudopsychics from wanting to become involved in research[2] but have the

---

2. This may not always be the case. Some researchers may actually wish to work with pseudopsychics. For example, researchers may wish to study the strategies of deception employed by such individuals. Alternatively researchers may believe that a specific pseudopsychic is harmful to the general public and should be exposed as a fake. If this is the case researchers

opposite effect on honest claimants (i.e., individuals who do not intend to deceive researchers).

Deterring the Pseudopsychic

This section will outline some research policies designed to deter pseudopsychics from wanting to become involved in research. Much of the work in this section is based upon Morris (1986a).

First, pseudopsychics should be persuaded that if they become involved in research, they are likely to be exposed as fraudulent. This is best done by persuading potential claimants that investigators are skilled at countering psychic fraud. To achieve this it is important that researchers actually do possess expertise at countering psychic fraud, and that this is clearly conveyed to the claimant. This can be achieved in several ways. Any recommended reading lists produced by researchers could contain standard texts on conjuring and psychic fraud. In addition, potential claimants could be informed about the general types of expertise (such as that possessed by magicians, security experts, etc.) that have been, and may be, consulted to help design and run studies. However, researchers should guard against inadvertently giving away any information that might enable the pseudopsychic to anticipate, and thus overcome, the controls used during experimentation.

---

should obviously not insist on any policies which would deter a pseudo psychic from becoming involved in research.

Second, pseudopsychics should be persuaded that there will be little reward for deceiving researchers, even if such cheating should go undetected. To achieve this, it is important to understand the various factors that motivate pseudopsychics to deceive (see chapter 2). To counter such motivation, researchers could consider instigating the following research policies. To prevent pseudopsychics from being motivated by financial reward, researchers should avoid paying claimants anything other than a token amount of money (e.g., to cover expenses) for their involvement in testing. Many of the rewards outlined in chapter 2 (e.g., increased business, attention, and personal power) depend upon the claimant being able to publicize his or her involvement with researchers. To counter this, researchers could adopt a policy of not allowing claimants to discuss a study with the media until a specified time after its completion. This policy may also help avoid the "media circus" that has dogged some past investigations. Finally, potential claimants could also be informed that research policy dictates that all reports of an investigation will not include the name of the claimant, unless (perhaps) the claimant has been shown to be fraudulent.

Third, a pseudopsychic should be persuaded that there will be negative consequences if he or she is caught cheating during an investigation. For example, investigators could inform potential claimants that any evidence of cheating may be described in parapsychology journals, popular magazines, and newspapers. In addition, such reports may carry the name of the claimant, and this information would be circulated to other researchers. In addition, the negative social consequences of being labeled a cheat could be emphasized to all potential claimants.

Motivating Honest Claimants

Honest claimants (i.e., individuals who do not intend to deceive researchers) should be encouraged to become involved in research. This can be achieved in several ways. First, the policies should outline the theoretical and practical benefits that might flow from parapsychologists understanding the nature of ostensible psychic functioning. For example, researchers could stress the social good that could come from a thorough understanding of ostensible psychic detective work and healing. Second, genuine claimants may consider some of the research policies described in the section above to be overcomplicated, unnecessary, and possibly even offensive. This problem can be tackled in several ways. The document could briefly describe some previous instances of psychic fraud, outlining the damage caused by such trickery (see chapter 1). This may help honest claimants appreciate why researchers are taking the issue of subject cheating so seriously. The document should briefly explain why each of the research policies act to deter the pseudopsychic. The document should stress that an honest claimant has nothing to fear from such measures and that there is no possibility of them being unfairly labeled a cheat. Indeed, the document should note that such policies exist, in part, to help protect honest claimants being unfairly criticized by skeptics who may otherwise fault a study after its completion.

5

Pilot Studies

If researcher and claimant do decide to work together, pilot studies should be run before any formal experimentation. These studies should be designed to both act as an initial assessment of the claimant and also help with the design of more formal testing.

Early pilot studies should maximize the opportunity for the claimant to demonstrate his or her psychic ability. The researcher should conform, as far as is practically possible, to the conditions that the claimant believes to be conducive. If, under such circumstances, the claimant is unable to produce any unusual phenomena, researchers may decide not to invest additional resources in more formal experimentation. If, however, the claimant manages to produce something of interest, the claimant could be assured that more formal experimentation will follow. Researchers should inform claimants of these facts before any pilot sessions take place. Ideally, this agreement should take the form of a short written agreement signed by both researcher and claimant.

Pilot studies should be designed, and recorded, to aid in the development of more formal experimentation. For example, some writers (e.g., Morris 1986a; Hansen 1990) have noted that the design of an experimental protocol may be improved by researchers interacting with magicians. Morris (1986a) has noted how this interaction may be helped by magicians either observing the claimant in person, or viewing a videotape of the claimant. Pilot studies could act as an opportunity for magicians to witness the claimant, and for researchers to obtain videotape of his or her demonstrations.

Pilot studies can also give researchers an opportunity to assess some of the controls that might be used in more formal experimentation. For example, the researcher may wish to film the claimant during future experiments. If this is the case, pilot studies can be an ideal opportunity to explore the best way of carrying out such filming (e.g., how far the camera should be from the claimant, what the best angle for filming is, and so on). This introduction and development of potential controls may also help the claimant appreciate some of the conditions under which formal experimentation will occur. This, in turn, may act to sharpen a claim, should certain controls inhibit the production of phenomena.

Finally, as mentioned earlier, before undertaking pilot studies researchers should clearly inform claimants that any phenomena produced during such studies would not be taken as evidence of psychic ability. This may help avoid a claimant erroneously believing (and telling others) that he or she has been formally tested when, in reality, only a pilot investigation has been conducted.

6

Formal Research

Initial research usually tries to discover whether a claimant can produce convincing evidence to support his or her apparent psychic ability. This type of research is labeled "proof-oriented," because it investigates the validity of the phenomena in question. If this initial work is promising, researchers may then wish to try to identify factors, such as the psychological state of the claimant, the distance between claimant and target, that either enhance or diminish the claimant's ability. This latter type of research is known as "process-oriented" because it is an attempt to determine the processes that govern the phenomena (see chapter 8).

There are four general stages involved in the planning of formal studies:

Step 1
Decide on a general design for an experiment.

Step 2

Figure out all of the ways in which the results of that experiment could be explained by normal (i.e., nonpsychic) explanations.

Step 3

Develop controls to minimize the possibility of these explanations.

Step 4

Ensure that the claimant believes that he or she will be able to be "psychic" during the experiment.

The following four sections discuss these steps in more detail.

Step 1: An Initial Design

Many readers will be aware of the basic experimental designs used within parapsychology, and of how these designs can be used to form the basis of a wide range of experiments. This section is intended for readers who do not have a background in experimental parapsychology and briefly introduces some of the main stages involved in ESP and PK tests. Further information on this topic is available in several standard parapsychology texts (see Appendix A).

TESTING FOR EXTRASENSORY PERCEPTION (ESP)

The following six stages are usually involved in ESP testing.

1. A target is randomly selected from a group of possible targets (referred to as the "target pool").

2. A set of barriers is erected to prevent normal channels of communication between target and claimant.

3. The claimant attempts to psychically divine the identity of the target. In tests of telepathy the target is known to another individual. In tests of clairvoyance no individual is aware of the target's identity. This stage of testing may be carried out in many ways. One main distinction is between "free response" and "forced choice" studies. In free response studies the claimant is unaware of the identity of the targets in the target pool and only knows the type of thing that the target might be (any picture, any object, any geographical location, etc.) The claimant is asked to describe, or draw, any ideas or images ("mentation") that come to mind during the response period. In forced choice studies the claimant is aware of the identity of each potential target in the target pool and informs the experimenter of his or her guess as to which has been chosen as the target.

4. An individual (referred to as a "judge") has to decide which member of the target pool best corresponds with the claimant's mentation. In free response studies the judge (who may either be the claimant or another individual) is shown members of the target pool (including, of course, the actual target) and is asked to decide which target best corresponds with the claimant's mentation.

5. In the next stage of testing the actual target is compared with the target chosen by the judge in the previous

stage. The claimant scores a "hit" if the two targets match and a "miss" if they do not.

6. In the final stage researchers have to calculate the statistical significance of the number of hits obtained by the claimant.

The stages described above relate to claims of clairvoyance or telepathy. The steps involved in precognition are almost identical, except that the order of the events is reversed, with the claimant attempting to predict the identity of the target *before* it has been selected.

An Example: Testing for Clairvoyance

Let us imagine that an individual approaches researchers claiming clairvoyant ability. A standard "free response" test of such a claim might proceed as follows. Researchers first select four pictures (e.g., postcards) to act as a target pool. Each of these pictures is placed into an opaque envelope and the four envelopes shuffled. Researchers then randomly select one of the envelopes to act as a "target" [*Stage 1*]. This target envelope is placed somewhere secure (e.g., into a locked drawer) while the remaining three envelopes are placed into a separate, but equally secure, location [*Stage 2*]. The claimant is then asked to draw, or describe, his or her mentation concerning the target picture [*Stage 3*]. Next, the claimant is shown (or sent, if the test is being carried out by post) a copy of each picture in the target pool and asked to choose the picture that best matches the mentation [*Stage 4*]. The researchers then look into the target envelope and discover which of the four pictures was the actual target. If the claimant previously selected this picture as the best match he or she has scored a "hit." If they selected any other potential target picture then they have scored a "miss" [*Stage 5*]. The above procedure constitutes one trial. Obviously, no strong conclusions can be drawn from just a single trial. However, if this test were to be repeated several times, simple statistical analyses could be used to investigate the degree to which the claimant's performance deviates away from chance (see Edge, Morris, Palmer, and Rush 1986) [*Stage 6*].

TESTING FOR PSYCHOKINESIS (PK)

The two types of PK have already been described: in macro-PK the claimant attempts to influence a static object (e.g., a piece of cutlery) or a system that has relatively stable properties (e.g., the temperature of a room); in micro-PK the claimant attempts to influence a statistical system, such as the roll of a die or output of a random number generator (RNG). The issues involved in testing micro-PK are conceptually identical to those involved in evaluating precognition. The difference between the two is only one of apparent causation. Whereas in precognition the claimant appears to be predicting the outcome of a freely determined event, in micro-PK the claimant appears to be making the event conform to his or her volition.

There are four steps involved in most tests of macro-PK.

1. Researchers first examine the object(s), or area, that will later be involved in testing. Such examination can take several forms, depending upon the type of macro-PK being evaluated. For example, when assessing a medium's claim of materialization, researchers may wish to ensure that the séance room does not contain any hidden objects. In contrast, when evaluating claims of spoon bending, researchers usually carefully examine the cutlery to ensure that it has not been tampered with beforehand. When testing claims of telekinesis researchers should ensure that there are no concealed mechanisms or devices (e.g., threads, magnets) that could be used to apply a force to the target.

2. Barriers are then erected to prevent the claimant influencing the target by normal means. For example, when assessing claims of materialization researchers may wish to ensure that the claimant does not smuggle any objects into the room. In contrast, when testing claims of dematerialization researchers should ensure that the claimant cannot smuggle the target out of the room.

3. Next, the claimant is asked to psychically influence the target.

4. Finally, researchers reexamine the object, or area, and decide whether any ostensible macro-PK has occurred. Again, this reexamination can take several forms. For example, when assessing an apparent dematerialization researchers may attempt to ensure that the dematerialized target is not hidden in the room.When testing apparent PK

spoon bending researchers may closely examine the piece of cutlery to ensure that it has actually changed shape.

Step 2: Anticipating Possible Trickery

Researchers should try to figure out all of the biases and artifacts that could ruin an experiment. Many of the most frequently occurring problems have already been described in standard texts on methods within psychology and parapsychology (see Appendix A). Researchers are advised to study these texts before embarking upon any experimentation. Investigators testing psychic claimants face a special problem, as they have to try to think of ways in which a claimant might attempt to cheat during testing. This section is designed to help researchers tackle this problem.

GENERAL TYPES OF CHEATING

As a starting point, researchers may find it helpful to think of how the following types of cheating categorization (based upon Morris 1986a) might be attempted by a pseudopsychic during testing.

For ESP tests:

1. Could a pseudopsychic bias the selection of the target?
2. Could a pseudopsychic discover the nature of the target by reconstructing its selection procedure?

3. Could a pseudopsychic switch the target after it has been selected?

4. Could a pseudopsychic monitor several potential targets, only revealing the one that matches his or her mentation?

5. Could a pseudopsychic gain access to other sources of information that describe the target (e.g., the remaining members of the target pool)?

6. Could the target be accessed before the barriers are in place?

7. Do the barriers effectively prevent information flowing between target and pseudopsychic?

8. Could the barriers be secretly removed and replaced?

9. Could the target be accessed after the barriers are removed?

10. Could a pseudopsychic switch his or her mentation after the target is revealed?

11. Could a pseudopsychic make many sets of mentation, but only reveal the one that matches the target after the target is revealed?

12. Could a pseudopsychic have biased the recording of the mentation to match the target?

13. Could the comparison of the claimant's guess and target be biased?

For macro-PK testing:

1. Will the initial examination of the target object and area be sufficient to detect any signs of trickery?

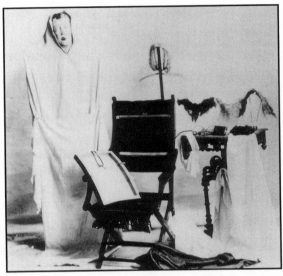

Apparatus used by Charles Eldred, a fraudulent medium working around the turn of the century. *Mary Evans Picture Library/The Harry Price Collection, University of London.*

2. What normal methods could be used to influence the target?

3. Will the barriers prevent these methods?

4. Could a pseudopsychic influence the target before or after the barriers are in place?

5. Could the barriers be secretly removed and replaced?

6. Will the reexamination of the target or target area be sufficient to detect any signs of trickery?

FORMING MORE SPECIFIC IDEAS

To form additional ideas about possible methods of trickery, researchers could take the following steps.

Consult past parapsychological literature

Researchers could search previous parapsychological literature to discover whether past studies have assessed the type of claim currently being evaluated (see Appendix A). Relevant literature may help researchers appreciate the specific types of trickery that they may encounter during their investigation.

Consult with magicians

Researchers should consider consulting with magicians. This can have both advantages and disadvantages. On the positive side, researchers may benefit from magicians' knowledge of conjuring and psychic fraud. In addition, magicians may be more skilled than lay observers at identifying novel forms of trickery. However, researchers should be aware that magicians can themselves be fooled. Indeed, there is an entire branch of magic that aims only to fool magicians and is referred to as "magic for magicians." In short, magicians are perhaps best viewed as useful consultants but should not be relied upon to design a completely fraud-proof experiment.

When selecting a consultant magician, researchers should be aware that most magicians specialize in certain types of magic and thus be careful to choose someone with appropriate expertise. Researchers may also find it helpful to understand some of the barriers that, in the past, have hindered communication between researcher and magicians. Hansen (1990) cites many such factors, including, researchers' lack of knowledge of conjuring, the clandestine nature of magical literature, the absence of an established network of communication between researchers and magicians, and the false belief that magicians are hostile to parapsychology. Also, researchers should be aware that some magicians may be interested in self-publicity and may wish to involve the media in testing. This, coupled with a claimant who enjoys such attention, could severely disrupt testing. Some of these problems could be minimized by researchers joining local, national, and international magic societies (see Appendix B) and attending magic conventions.

Consult the conjuring/pseudopsychic literature

Researchers should also study some of the publications that outline relevant methods of conjuring and psychic fraud (see Appendix A). It is not necessary that researchers become expert in all areas of psychic fraud. Instead, they should aim to form a good general understanding of the topic and a more detailed knowledge of tricks that are more relevant to the claim under investigation.

Consult with technical specialists

When a claimant wishes to try to influence complex target systems (e.g., a computer, the human body) researchers should discover how such systems could be secretly influenced by a pseudopsychic. This may involve interacting with individuals who understand these types of systems more fully (e.g., computer experts, physiologists, etc.).

ASSESSING THE PLAUSIBILITY OF FRAUDULENT METHODS

Researchers should be wary of incorrectly rejecting certain types of trickery as being implausible. This section outlines two of the most common reasons for erroneous rejection.

"But the claimant just isn't that skilled at trickery."

Researchers may reject a trick as implausible if they do not believe the claimant capable of such fraud. For example, the claimant may not appear to have the physical strength, dexterity, or knowledge of conjuring required to perform a certain type of trickery.

However, this appearance may be deceptive in two ways. First, researchers may be deceived into underestimating the claimant's conjuring skill or physical abilities. Second, researchers may overestimate the necessary skill needed to carry out a certain trick. For example, researchers may assume that a certain sleight-of-hand would take many years to perfect when, in reality, this is not the case. This problem can be minimized in several ways. Ideally, researchers should devise tests that, if they are to be overcome, call for extreme competence and resources. If this is not possible, researchers should attempt to determine whether the claimant possesses the expertise to carry out the trickery needed to overcome proposed controls.

When doing this, researchers should allow themselves a safe margin of error. That is, they should consciously underestimate the expertise required to perform certain trickery, and overestimate the claimant's expertise for deception. This may appear unnecessarily cautious.

However, at a future date it may be discovered that a certain type of trickery is far easier than supposed. Alternatively, new evidence may reveal that a past claimant was indeed a more sophisticated trickster than assumed at the time of testing. Unless researchers have left themselves a safe margin of error their controls may, in retrospect, be seen as inadequate.

"But the claimant hasn't used, or been accused of using, that type of trickery in the past."

Researchers may reject an explanation as implausible if it does not entail the type of trickery that the claimant has used, or been accused of using, in the past. A pseudopsychic may exploit this assumption by developing a number of ways of fabricating a certain type of phenomenon, and then switching methods both within, and between, demonstrations. It is for this reason that many texts on magic, and psychic fraud, contain several different methods for achieving the same effect. Diaconis (1985) labels this approach the "bundle of sticks phenomenon," noting:

> An effect is produced several times under different circumstances with the use of a different technique each time . . . the weak points of one performance are ruled

out because they were clearly not present during other performances. The bundle of sticks is stronger than any single stick. (p. 572)

Tamariz (1988) notes that the success of this strategy rests on the fact that some individuals erroneously assume that "the same causes produce the same effects," rather than that a single effect may be produced by many, quite different, methods. The use of such multiple methods provides the pseudopsychic with several additional advantages over researchers. First, he or she can select a method to suit a given situation. Second, the deceiver also has the option of switching methods within a performance, should the use of one method become problematic. Magicians refer to such alternative methods as "outs." Third, researchers may suspect one particular method of trickery, look for it, see that they were wrong, and conclude that the effect is paranormal. Fourth, the pseudopsychic may repeatedly perform the same effect (with changing safeguards), always using a different method, to encourage researchers to conclude that, because no one method could account for all of the observed phenomena, the effect must be paranormal. In short, researchers should avoid developing any type of "mind set" that could lead them to erroneously reject a method as implausible simply because a claimant has not been accused of using such a method in the past.

Step 3: Countering Possible Trickery

The term "control" refers to any technique used during a study to detect or prevent trickery. This section outlines the types of controls available to researchers, and some of the issues surrounding their use.

BARRIERS AND DETECTORS

Some controls are designed to eliminate fraud from occurring ("barriers"), while others are designed to monitor its occurrence ("detectors"). The differences between these controls can be illustrated with a hypothetical example. Let us imagine that a claimant states that he or she is capable of psychically bending a spoon. To prevent the claimant from physically bending the spoon, researchers could, for example, place the spoon in a sealed test tube. If so, they would have placed a barrier around the target. Alternatively, researchers could use a video camera to film any instances in which the claimant handles the spoon, in the hope that such filming will detect any trickery. In this instance the video camera would act as a detector (i.e., it would detect, as oppose to prevent, possible fraud).

Some parapsychologists may fail to be impressed by any investigation that only uses detectors as controls. It has been argued that some claimants will cheat when given the opportunity to do so, and only resort to using genuine psychic ability when prevented from being fraudulent. Individuals finding this reasoning compelling believe that the only correct way to test such claimants is to prevent, rather than detect, fraud. In addition, researchers using only barriers will, at the end of testing, only be able to decide whether the claimant has displayed ostensible psychic ability. In contrast, researchers employing detectors may be able to tell both whether the claimant displayed psychic ability, and whether he or she attempted some form of trickery. However, this decision may be far from straightforward, as it is often difficult to decide whether such evidence constitutes proof of actual cheating. For example, Collins and Pinch (1982) report accusing a claimant of faking spoon bending, basing their belief on the evidence of a single photograph. The photograph showed the claimant holding the spoon in both hands, with each hand at one end of the spoon. However, the claimant attempted to explain this photograph away, stating that it was taken as she passed the spoon from one hand to another.

Pseudopsychics can exploit this difficulty in two ways. First, they may manipulate researchers into selecting controls that result in ambiguous evidence of fraud. As noted above, it has sometimes proved problematic to unambiguously accuse a claimant of fraud based on a single photograph. A pseudopsychic knowing this may encourage researchers to control against fraud by using a still camera to photograph the experiment, knowing what they can get away with. Second, the pseudopsychic may prepare several excuses to instantly explain away any evidence of fraud that is likely to be discovered by researchers. For example, Randi (1987) reports that Dr P. J. Lincoln (a specialist in blood group serology and forensic medicine at London Hospital Medical College) investigated the claims being made by Filipino psychic surgeons. Lincoln surreptitiously obtained some of the apparently "bad tissue" removed from a patient by an alleged psychic surgeon, and analyzed it. Lincoln discovered that the blood sample was from a cow, and that the "tumor" was a piece of chicken intestine. However, the surgeons attempted to explain away this evidence stating that it was a well-known fact that "supernatural forces" convert the tumors into innocuous substances once they have left the patient's body.

For these reasons, researchers should only use detectors that produce relatively unambiguous evidence of cheating. When assessing this aspect of their controls researchers should try to figure out as many ways as possible in which apparent evidence of trickery could be produced by nonfraudulent causes. In this way the honest claimant will not suffer the indignity of unfairly being labeled a cheat, and the pseudopsychic will find it more difficult to explain away evidence of actual trickery. This may be problematic but the task may be eased by researchers examining past studies that have either tested the same claim, employed similar controls, or assessed the claimant in question. Such studies may give an insight into some of the problems and potential "outs" that have arisen in these situations.

OPEN AND HIDDEN CONTROLS

A second distinction concerns "open" and "hidden" controls. The nature of an "open" control is known to the claimant. As noted above, researchers may wish to detect a claimant applying physical force to a piece of cutlery. To do so, researchers may inform the claimant that any moments during which he or she handles the spoon will be closely filmed. If this were the case, such filming would constitute an open control. A "hidden" control, such as a secret camera, is concealed from the claimant.

The use of hidden controls can be problematic. Such controls can easily be made ineffective if the pseudopsychic can anticipate them. For this reason researchers should take special care to ensure that any information that describes the nature of these controls is unavailable to the claimant. In addition, a claimant may state that he or she finds it more psi conducive to know about all aspects of an experiment. The use of hidden controls would make such openness problematic. This, in turn, can make it difficult for claimants to predict whether or not they believe that they will be able to be "psychic" during the experiment (see step 4). Ideally, the best compromise would be to employ open controls that cannot easily be overcome, despite the fact that the claimant knows of their existence.

One of the most common types of detectors entails researchers simply observing a claimant. This is also one of the most problematic, because skilled tricksters can easily manipulate the attention of an observer. For example, pseudopsychics employ a wide range of techniques designed to lower the intensity of observers' attention. Fuller (1975) advises pseudopsychics to take a long time before attempting any form of trickery, because this time lag lowers observers' overall vigilance. Alternatively, the pseudopsychic may reduce observers' attention by acting as if the demonstration hasn't started yet, or has finished but been unsuccessful. Observers naturally reduce their attention during these moments and may miss any trickery performed at these times. A pseudopsychic may also manipulate the direction of observers' attention, steering it away from areas in which they are likely to detect trickery. Fitzkee (1945) has presented a good overview of some of the techniques used by magicians to misdirect observers' attention. The magician may, for example, divert an observer's attention by the use of movement, eye contact, or body language to deflect an observer's attention away from trickery. Pseudopsychics may also attempt to dull attention by confusing an observer. For example, Fuller (1975), in his advice to pseudopsychics, notes:

> When you're working for a group, keep talking, and moving fast. Create maximum chaos. Flit from one task to another. Fail on one thing, put it aside, try something else, then (yo back and try again, and so on. (p.15)

In short, researchers should show great care when only relying upon their observational abilities to detect trickery.

THE SECURITY INDUSTRY

When designing controls, researchers might find it helpful to consult with individuals involved in the security industry. Such people may possess useful information relating to the way in which criminals access supposedly secure systems, and they can advise researchers on commercial products that are designed to counter such trickery. Appendix C describes several products that may be particularly useful when testing psychic claimants.

WHICH CONTROLS SHOULD BE USED?

There is almost no general advice that can be given here. However, researchers may find it helpful to consider including a mixture of types of controls in their studies. This mixture could be designed to detect types of fraud that cannot easily be prevented, and vice versa.

Step 4: Negotiating an Experimental Protocol

Researchers have to ensure that claimants believe that they will be able to produce phenomena under the conditions being proposed.

Such agreement is important for two reasons. First, if honest claimants do not agree with the conditions in advance, and fail to produce any apparent evidence of psychic ability during the experiment, they may legitimately claim that they have been unfairly tested. Second, if pseudopsychics did not agree to the conditions of the experiment, and fail to fake psychic ability during that experiment, they may claim that the experimental conditions were not conducive to their ability. For example, Eugene Burger (1986) notes that if a fake medium is unable to fabricate phenomena, he or she can state, "Well, my friends, conditions sometimes are just not right for this sort of thing." Burger notes:

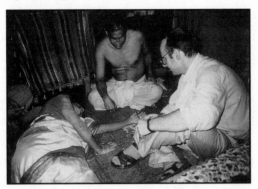

The first author (right) investigating an Indian religious leader (Minu Bhowmick) who claimed both trance and macro-PK ability.

> You see . . . there's always an "out"—a non-humiliat-ing, non-embarrassing, perfectly reasonable (given the folk-accepted assumptions about séances and how they "work"), perfectly acceptable out for a failure. (p. 107)

As a result, the experiment may be discounted as incon-clusive rather than being perceived as evidence against the claimant possessing psychic ability.

Developing such a protocol can be problematic for many reasons. Researchers may find themselves unwilling to inform the claimant about the exact nature of the con-trols that will be used in the experiment. If this is the case, the claimant may not know the exact conditions under which he or she will be expected to perform. There are some steps that can be taken to minimize this problem. Researchers could attempt to design, and employ, controls that are not likely to prevent psychic functioning. This could entail, in part, developing noninvasive controls. For example, if a claimant feels awkward when being filmed during an experiment, researchers could consider the use of hidden (and therefore less invasive) cameras. Researchers could also secretly introduce controls into pilot studies to determine whether they inhibit the production of the claimant's ability.

The process of protocol development can entail a considerable amount of back-and-forth communication between claimant and researcher. Pseudopsychics may attempt to exploit this process by negotiating away any controls that they believe effectively counter psychic fraud. If researchers are not wise to this stratagem, they can be unwittingly manipulated into accepting these conditions, not realizing that such alterations aid the deception process. For example, Randi (1983a) describes how in Project Alpha, the two pseudopsychics complained about electronic equipment putting out "bad vibes," such that the researchers were not able to videotape the demonstrations. In addition, Eugene Burger (1986) recounts how fake mediums insist that all of. the sitters must link hands, often in a dark room, during a séance. The fake medium may state that this is necessary to bring forth spirit communication. In reality it is designed to prevent curious sitters from reaching out into the séance room and discovering various forms of trickery (such as secret apparatus and accomplices). It is vital that researchers closely monitor, and record, every step of the negotiation process. Essentially, they should make quite certain that any negotiated changes have not altered the chances of a claimant being able to successfully fake psychic ability.

Despite such difficulties it is vital that both researcher, and claimant, fully understand and are satisfied with the experimental conditions. To help this process researchers should produce a clearly worded protocol that explicitly covers all of the major aspects of the proposed study. This might include, for example, the overall aims of the study, the experimental conditions, and a description of how the different possible results of the study will be worded and disseminated. In addition, it should contain a statement to the effect that the claimant agrees with the conditions, and believes them to be conducive to their abilities. Finally, researchers may also wish to include a written statement that notes that the claimant will not attempt to cheat during the experiment. Researchers should ask their claimants to sign this agreement before taking part in the formal testing. Such an agreement will help the assessment process in several ways. First, it will help ensure that, if claimants fall to produce any evidence of psychic ability, they cannot say that they did not fully understand the experimental conditions, or that such conditions were not psi conducive. Second, the protocol may help avoid any confusion that might arise after a study concerning when, where, and how the results of that study can be communicated to others. Obviously, it is vital that the claimant fully understands the nature of this written agreement. To help this process the agreement should be clearly written and talked through with the claimant.

To help the claimant appreciate the experimental conditions, researchers may also find it helpful to "walk" a claimant through a dry run of the experiment. Researchers could also give the claimant examples of how the report would describe the possible outcomes of the experiment, and of where such a report would be circulated.

7

Reporting Recommendations

When reporting a study, it is vital that researchers present a description that is complete, unambiguous, and reliable. Given that investigators may not be aware of the possible questions that may be raised once the study is published, it is important that they try to provide as full a description as possible.

Researchers should describe their initial interactions with a claimant. This may include how the claimant contacted the researcher (or vice versa), and details of the initial claim. The researcher should then describe any informal sessions and pilot studies undertaken with the claimant. This description should include details of how a claim was modified during this period, if such was the case. In addition, reports should also include verbatim copies of any agreements made between claimant and researcher.

Researchers should also fully describe the design of the experiment. They should state the types of trickery and bias taken into account before the experiment, and present the controls designed to counter these problems. The report should also include a full description of the stages involved in developing a mutually agreed protocol, with a verbatim copy of the final document.

Third, researchers should note whether the experiment proceeded according to plan. If this was not the case, researchers should describe any deviations away from the intended procedure, and comment upon the effect that these deviations may have on the assessment procedure. In addition, the researcher should describe, and assess, any evidence of possible fraud discovered during the investigation.

Fourth, researchers should attempt to help individuals who, at a later date, may wish to assess the investigation. Researchers should try to ensure that these individuals are able to inspect the actual equipment used during the experiment. Researchers should also attempt to record the study using many different types of media (e.g., still photographs, film, videotape, verbal descriptions, drawings, and plans). In this way the possibility of such evidence containing ambiguities is minimized. Also, when reporting a study researchers can base their descriptions on this evidence, and do not have to depend upon memory, which is more likely to be influenced by the effects of bias and decay.

Finally, to assess whether a report contains enough information, researchers could ask other individuals (especially those not directly involved in the study) to examine and assess the report. This can help researchers appreciate the quantity and quality of information needed in a well-written and convincing report.

8

Proof versus
Process-Oriented Research

Many researchers distinguish between research oriented toward proof of the existence of psychic functioning, or direct evaluation of some claim for special psychic abilities, versus research oriented toward understanding psychic processes, or "how psi works." The proof-oriented approach may emphasize studies done under conditions designed to rule out all non-psi explanations for any positive results that might occur, such as to constitute persuasive evidence to fair skeptics. The process-oriented approach may involve the systematic variation of conditions in order to test hypotheses about factors that influence success rates, such as individual differences in cognitive or personality characteristics; internal states such as those produced by drugs, suggestion, and so on; environmental differences, including social as well as physical factors; differences in the nature of the target; and differences in the nature of the barriers between the target and the participant who is being tested.

Both research strategies are valid and have their place. Both are amenable to fraud, although strategies for faking process-oriented research may be slightly more complex than those for proof-oriented, and it has been argued that successful lines of process-oriented research provide stronger forms of evidence than straightforward proof-oriented work. Since much of the business of serious science involves the study of process, it is important for us to consider the reasoning behind the process-oriented as well as the proof-oriented, how such reasoning can be exploited by frauds, and how such exploitation can be minimized.

Proof of the existence of psi in an absolute sense is difficult if not impossible, as one can always speculate about artifacts or fraud strategies that have been overlooked. But by paying careful attention to details and the issues raised previously, one can build a strong case for the claims of specific individuals. That case becomes strongest under the following circumstances:

1. The effect can be shown in the presence of a variety of investigators (including those with knowledge of fraud techniques) who are allowed considerable access to the testing conditions.
2. Detailed descriptions of procedures are publicly available and have been scrutinized for alternative possibilities without success.
3. Other participants produce the effect as well.
4. Factors which affect the strength of results can be identified.
5. Such factors start to generate models about what is

going on, with testable predictions. These models may involve physical, biological, or psychological variables.

Most of what has been presented in earlier sections deals with the first three points, especially the first two. They are proof-oriented: get the effect, ensure it's real, make sure it has no obvious non-psi interpretation. Now we consider the last two, involving the use of special claimants in research that compares results under different conditions, in order to explore the processes involved.

Deliberate Production of Patterns in Results

Claimants who are able to cheat can choose when to cheat, how to cheat, and when not to cheat, thus producing patterns in the results that may impress researchers, especially if they confirm their hypotheses.

CORRELATIONAL PATTERNS

Such patterns may involve physical, physiological, or psychological data being monitored repeatedly or continuously, such as to produce correlations with changes in psi performance.

Example: Suppose I am a pseudopsychic working with an investigator who expects strong positive psi results during periods of low, rather than high, geomagnetic activity. Each morning I find out the geomagnetic readings, perhaps by consulting available computerized databases. When they indicate low activity, I cheat during that day's session to produce strong positive psi results. When they are high, I either don't cheat or I cheat to ensure that my results are completely at chance (or perhaps even below chance, depending on my understanding of whether psi missing is of interest to the investigator). My results will correlate nicely with geomagnetic measurements, to whatever degree I might wish.

Example: Suppose I am being physiologically monitored. In exploratory sessions that the experimenter is conducting to get me adjusted to the equipment, I learn what variables are of interest to the researcher (heart rate, respiration rate, muscle activity, etc.); I practice how to control them, perhaps by thinking about exciting or arousing situations, putting myself through relaxation procedures or "safe harbor" imagery, and so on. I then cheat so as to produce my strongest psi results during those sessions in which I have also deliberately induced whatever levels of arousal my researcher most wants to be associated with psi hitting.

Example: My researcher asks me to fill out questionnaires before and after each session regarding my mood, confidence level, and so on. When I fill them out one way (happy mood, high confidence), I cheat to ensure strong positive results. When I fill them out the opposite way (low mood, low confidence), I cheat to produce strong negative results. When I fill them out neutrally (average mood or confidence), I cheat to make sure my psi performance is very close to chance.

Example: I may decide to combine variables, to produce a more complete pattern. For instance, if I learn that geomagnetic activity is low on Tuesday, I may make sure that my imagery that day is both bizarre and accurate (e.g., my confederate lets me know the target picture shows seagulls in flight, so I report many giant white birds dancing with mermaids under the sea, etc.). This pattern supports the researcher's model, that (for instance) low geomagnetic activity facilitates labile, unconstrained mentation which is more likely to facilitate the emergence of psychic information into consciousness.

Patterns Related to Deliberately Manipulated Conditions

Fraudulently produced patterns may also involve systematic variations in conditions made by the experimenter. The claimant learns what the researcher's expectations are and then tries to match them, for example, by producing strong results during the preferred conditions and weak results during the conditions of less interest to the experimenters.

Example: During half of the sessions the experimenter attempts to hypnotize me and during the other half I am merely asked to take some deep breaths and get relaxed. I pretend to be hypnotized, and make sure that I produce strong results during those sessions and chance results under the mere self-relaxation condition since the latter is obviously a control condition, of less interest to the researcher.

If I don't know which conditions are of most interest to the researchers, I may deliberately produce a mild difference between the conditions early on, and see if I get any cues from how pleased the researchers are. If they are pleased, I increase the strength of results in the same direction; if displeased I reverse the effect to see if they become happier. Even if I don't get any firm cues, I can continue to favor one condition with good results, thereby producing a clear pattern which is bound to be of interest to the researchers regardless of whether it matches a prediction of theirs. As we know, many researchers will become enthusiastic over any pattern they find; indeed, this is not an unreasonable attitude because it is well known that some very good science has been done by researchers who obtained results quite counter to their initial expectations.

Example: I am given two batches of seeds whose germination rates I am to influence by handling them. I acquire substitutes for one batch, which I damage in advance, I then exchange them surreptitiously for the target seeds of that batch during the sessions. These then germinate more slowly than the others. If my researchers are pleased, I damage the next batch even more. If they are not pleased, I acquire substitutes for the other batch of seeds and try damaging and exchanging them instead, to produce a differential effect in the opposite direction.

Patterns of results can also involve conditions not necessarily of initial interest to the researchers, conditions not being formally measured. For instance, I may decide to produce better results on rainy days, or when I am near metal, or there's an attractive person in the room with me, or after an excellent meal, and so on. If the researcher does not notice, after a few sessions I can call attention to the pattern myself. Or I may myself suggest that we could try giving me a fine meal before each session, to see what effect it might have.

Unintentional Fraudulent Pattern Production

Some patterns in results may be produced without conscious intent by pseudopsychics, simply because their method of cheating works better under certain conditions than others.

Example: I am asked to do psychic readings of several people, and unknown to me these people have all taken a battery of personality tests. I am a skilled muscle-reader, and am relying upon nonverbal cues to give me initial information as well as feedback regarding my statements. Some clients are more responsive nonverbally and some wear clothing, cologne, etc. that convey useful information about themselves. If these client differences correlate with personality measures then my results may well show (for instance) that I am better at reading people who are high in extraversion and openness, a pattern I did not even know was being explored.

Example: I am asked to bend strips of metal made of different materials. An accomplice arranges to pre-bend each strip, but some bend more easily than others, and some the accomplice leaves alone because they are known to produce tell-tale cracks if one attempts pre-bending. Thus when I attempt to produce bends during a test session by gentle stroking, some materials will show more of a bend than others, thereby producing patterns of results linked with metallurgical variables that I did not necessarily plan for. Comparably, some bending strategies may involve palming or otherwise temporarily concealing the test sample. If some kinds of samples are too large, then there will be results only with sufficiently small samples. Whatever other attributes are linked with test sample dimensions will therefore appear to be correlated with amenability to PK influence.

Guarding against Fraudulent Pattern Production

There really are no special techniques for safeguarding against fraudulent pattern production in process-oriented research. One must guard against fraud as best one can, even in process-oriented research, and not assume that the presence of patterns in findings are in and of themselves evidence against fraud. Certainly, researchers should do their best where feasible to conceal information from claimants about what hypotheses are being tested, as a matter of good general experimental procedure to prevent biases. A genuine psychic who knows what conditions the researcher favors may be more motivated to produce better results and may have greater expectation of success under those favored conditions.

Similarly, if experimental variables are being manipulated to test hypotheses, these manipulations should not be evident to claimants. Such information should be safeguarded in the same way as information about the target itself. Otherwise, any patterns found may be due to selective fraud from pseudopsychics or innocent bias from genuine psychically talented people.

In addition, if the researcher is in a position to delegate to another experimenter the data collection and interactions with claimants, then it may be possible to keep that experimenter blind to the experimental hypotheses, thus reducing the likelihood that the claimant may receive cues about these hypotheses.

When working with specific individuals claiming strong psychic ability, one should be cautious as well in interpreting any unanticipated patterns in results, because they may be intentional. If so, such patterns can serve as inadvertent clues pointing the alert researcher toward a fraudulent strategy in use. If results are better with small objects, for instance, this may suggest that a technique is being used that does not work with large objects, such as temporary palming and replacement. If researchers form hypotheses about a particular fraud technique being used, they may be able to vary conditions without the claimant knowing of it, to test out these hypotheses. How to do this would vary greatly from situation to situation, and would be in part up to the ingenuity of those involved.

In summary, it is dangerous to draw strong inferences about psychic processes from research with just one or two special claimants. It is better to look for similarities in patterns of results across many individuals. The more people who show a specific pattern the less likely it is to be the product of fraud, just as large numbers help ensure against some other artifacts. In general, for process-oriented research, the possibility of fraud can be treated very much like the possibility of other forms of artifact and bias. Good experimental procedure, common sense, and awareness of alternative interpretations are all necessary for meaningful process research, whether working with special claimants or any other population.

9

Conclusion

This manual has described several straightforward and simple techniques for minimizing the problems that can arise while testing psychic claimants. The first few sections of the manual outlined methods for identifying claimants who are particularly likely to be tricksters. The remainder of the manual dealt with the design, running, and reporting of experimentation. These latter sections have stressed the need for researchers to employ effective safeguards against potential subject cheating.

The manual has discussed the main issues involved in this type of work. However, there are several "satellite" areas that are not covered. For example, the manual does not discuss ways of handling the media interest that is usually generated by this type of research. Neither has it discussed strategies that can be used to locate potential claimants. It is hoped that future versions of the manual will include these and many other interesting issues. For the moment readers will have to be content with references to texts relating to these issues (see Appendix A).

A last note of warning: in this type of research it is especially true that a little knowledge is a dangerous thing. Some of the easiest individuals to fool are those who are very confident of their ability to detect deception. These guidelines will help minimize the possibility of subject deception: they are not (and probably can never be) absolutely foolproof. Genuine claimants present parapsychologists with a valuable opportunity to learn about psychic functioning. Dishonest claimants provide an excellent chance to investigate the psychology of deception. Either way, such work is both interesting and important. It is hoped that these guidelines will encourage researchers to carry out such work, and help them achieve the high methodological standards that their honest subjects fully deserve.

References

AUERBACH, L. *ESP, Hauntings and Poltergeists: A Para-psychologist's Handbook.* New York: Warner Books, 1986.

BATCHELDOR, K. J. "Report on a Case of Table Levitation and Associated Phenomena." *Journal of the Society for Psychical Research* 43 , 1966, 339–56.

BELOFF, J. "Research Strategies for Dealing with Unstable Phenomena." *Parapsychology Review* 15 (1), 1984, 1–21.

BELOFF, J. "Once a Cheat: Always a Cheat? Eusapia Palladino Revisited." *Proceedings of the Parapsychological Association 34th Annual Convention.* Heidelberg, Germany, 1991, 35–45.

BELOFF, J. *Parapsychology: A Concise History.* London: Athlone Press, 1993.

BRAUDE, S. E. *The Limits of Influence.* New York: Routledge and Kegan Paul Limited, 1986.

BURGER, E. *Spirit Theater.* New York: Kaufman and Greenberg, 1986.

COLLINS, H. M. "Magicians in the Laboratory: A New Role to Play." *New Scientist* 98, 1983, 929–31.

COLLINS, H. M., and T. J. PINCH. *Frames of Meaning. The Social Construction of Extraordinary Science.* London: Routledge and Kegan Paul Limited, 1982.

DELANOY, D. L. "Work with a Fraudulent PK Metal-bending Subject." *Journal of the Society for Psychical Research* 54, 1987, 247–56.

DELANOY, D. L., C. A. WATT, R. L. MORRIS, and R. WISEMAN. "A New Methodology for Free-response ESP Testing Outwith the Laboratory: Findings from Experienced Participants." *Proceedings of the Parapsychological Association 36th Annual Convention.* Toronto, Canada, 1993, 204–21.

DIACONIS, P. "Statistical Problems in ESP Research." In: *A Skeptics Handbook of Parapsychology.* Edited by P. Kurtz. Amherst, N.Y.: Prometheus Books, 1985, 569–84.

Edge, H. L., R. L. Morris, J. Palmer, and J. H. Rush. *Foundations of Parapsychology: Exploring the Boundaries of Human Capability.* Boston: Routledge and Kegan Paul, 1986.

FITZKEE, D. *The Trick Brain.* San Rafael, Calif.: San Rafael House, 1944.

FITZKEE, D. *Magic by Misdirection.* San Rafael, Calif.: San Rafael House, 1945.

FULLER, U. *Confessions of a Psychic.* Teaneck, N.J.: Karl Fulves, 1975.

HANSEN, G. P. "Deception by Subjects in Psi Research." *Journal of the American Society for Psychical Research* 84, 1990, 25–80.

KURTZ, P., ed. *A Skeptic's Handbook of Parapsychology.* Amherst, N.Y.: Prometheus Books, 1985.

MILLS, J. *Six Years with God.* New York: A and W Publishers, 1979.

MORRIS, R. L. "Minimizing Subject Fraud in Parapsychology Laboratories." *European Journal of Parapsychology* 6, 1986, 137–49.

PALMER, J. "Letter to the Editor." *Journal of the Society for Psychical Research* 55, 1988, 107–109.

RANDI, J. (1983a) "A Test of Psychokinetic Metal Bending: An Aborted Experiment" (Summary). In: W. G. Roll, J. Beloff, and R. A. White, eds., *Research in Parapsychology.* Metuchen, N.J.: Scarecrow Press Ltd., 1982, pp 112–13.

———. (1983b) The Project Alpha Experiment: Part 2; Beyond the Laboratory. *The Skeptical Inquirer* 8(1), 1983, 36–45.

———. *Flim-Flam! Psychics, ESP, Unicorns and other Delusions.* Amherst, N.Y.: Prometheus Books, 1987.

ROBERT-HOUDINI, J. E. *The Secrets of Conjuring and Magic.* (Translated and edited with notes by Professor Hoffman.) London, 1878.

SIDGWICK, E. "Introductory Note to 'The Report on Sittings with Eusapia Palladino.' " *Proceedings of the Society of Psychical Research* 23, 1909, 306–309.

TAMARIZ, J. *The Magic Way.* Madrid: Frakson Magic Books, 1988.

TIETZE, T. R. *Margery.* New York: Harper and Row, 1973.

Truzzi, M. "Reflections on 'Project Alpha': Scientific Experiment or Conjuror's Illusion?" *Zetetic Scholar* 12/13, 1987, 73–98.

Appendix A

Useful Literature

General Reading in Parapsychology

ALCOCK, J. *Parapsychology: Science or Magic? A Psychological Perspective.* Oxford: Pergamon Press, 1981.

BROUGHTON, R. *Parapsychology: The Controversial Science.* London: Rider Books, 1992.

COUTTIE, B. *Forbidden Knowledge: The Paranormal Paradox.* Cambridge: Lutterworth Press, 1988.

EDGE, H. L., R. L. MORRIS, J. PALMER, and J. H. RUSH. *Foundations of Parapsychology: Exploring the Boundaries of Human Capability.* Boston: Routledge and Kegan Paul, 1986.

EYSENCK, H. J., and C. SARGENT. *Explaining the Unerplained: Mysteries of the Paranormal.* London: Weidenfeld and Nicolson, 1982.

IRWIN, H. *Introduction to Parapsychology.* Jefferson, N.C.: McFarland, 1989.

KRIPPNER, S., ed. *Advances in Parapsychological Research.* Six volumes, most published by Jefferson, N.C.: McFarland, between 1977 and 1990.

KURTZ, P., ed. *A Skeptic's Handbook bf Parapsychology.* Amherst, N.Y.: Prometheus Books, 1985.

WOLMAN, B. B., ed. *Handbook of Parapsychology.* New York: Van Nostrand Reinhold, 1977.

General Reading on Experimental Design in Psychology

BARBER, T. X. *Pitfalls in Human Research.* New York: Pergamon Press, 1976.

BLACK, T. R. *Evaluating Social Science Research.* London: Sage Publications, 1993.

HARRIS, P. *Designing and Reporting Experiments.* Milton Keynes, UK: Open University Press. 1994.

LEECH, J. *Running Applied Psychology Experiments.* Milton Keynes, UK: Open University Press, 1991.

Specific Texts on Testing Psychic Claimants

AUERBACH, L. *ESP, Hauntings and Poltergeists: A Parapsychologist's Handbook.* New York: Warner Books, 1986.

———. "Stage Magic: What Do Parapsychologists Need to Know?" In D. H. Weiner and R. D. Nelson, eds., *Research in Parapsychology* 1986. Metuchen, N.J.: Scarecrow Press Ltd., 1987, pp. 182–85.

BAKER, R. A., and NICKELL, J. *Missing Pieces.* Amherst, N.Y.: Prometheus Books, 1992.

DINGWALL, E. *How to Go to a Medium.* London: Kegan Paul, 1927.

HANSEN, G. P. "Deception by Subjects in Psi Research." *Journal of the American Society for Psychical Research,* 84, 1990, 25–80.

———. "A Brief Overview of Magic for Parapsychologists." *Parapsychological Review,* 16(2), 1985, 5–8.

———. "Examples of a Need for Conjuring Knowledge." In D. H. Weiner and R. D. Nelson, eds., *Research in Parapsychology 1986.* Metuchen, N.J.: Scarecrow Press Ltd., 1987, pp. 185–86.

KOREM, D. *Powers: Testing the Psychic and Supernatural.* Intervarsity Press, 1988.

MORRIS, R. L. "Minimizing Subject Fraud in Parapsychology Laboratories." *European Journal of Parapsychology* 6, 1986, 137–49.

MORRIS, R. L. "What Psi is Not: The Necessity for Experiments." In H. L. Edge, R. L. Morris, J. H. Rush and J. Palmer, *Foundations of Parapsychology: Exploring the Boundaries of Human Capability.* Boston: Routledge and Kegan Paul, 1986, pp. 70–110.

WISEMAN, R., and R. L. MORRIS. "Modelling the Stratagems of Psychic Fraud." *European Journal of Parapsychology,* 1995, in press.

Additional Useful Texts within Psychology

HAMEL, J., S. DUFOUR, and D. FORTIN. *Case Study Methods.* London: Sage Publications, 1993.

LEE, R. M. *Doing Research on Sensitive Topics.* London: Sage Publications, 1993.

YIN, R. K. *Case Study Research.* Applied Social Research Methods series, Volume 5. London: Sage Publications, 1989.

Past Investigations of Claimants: Case Histories and Commentaries

BELOFF, J. *Parapsychology: a Concise History.* London: Athlone Press, 1993.

DELANOY, D. L. "Work with a Fraudulent PK Metal-bending Subject." *Journal of the Society for Psychical Research,* 54, 1987, 247–56.

FEILDING, E., W. W. BAGGALLY, and H. CARRINGTON. "Report on a Series of Sittings with Eusapia Palladino." *Proceedings of the Society for Psychical Research,* 23, 1909, 309–569.

GREGORY, A. *The Strange Case of Rudi Schneider.* Metuchen, N.J.: Scarecrow Press, 1985.

HARALDSSON, E. *Miracles Are My Visiting Cards.* London: Century Press, 1987.

MARKS, D. and R. KAMMANN. *The Psychology of the Psychic.* Amherst, N.Y.: Prometheus Books, 1980.

RANDI, J. *The Faith Healers.* Amherst, N.Y.: Prometheus Books, 1987.

WISEMAN, R., J. BELOFF, and R. L. MORRIS. "Testing the ESP Claims of SORRAT." *Journal of the Society for Psychical Research* 58, 1992, 363–77.

WISEMAN, R. and E. HARALDSSON. "Investigating Macro-PK in India: Swami Premananda." *Journal of the Society for Psychical Research* 58, 1995, in press.

Methods of Psychic Fraud and Conjuring

ABBOTT, D. P. *Behind the Scenes with the Medium.* Chicago, Ill.: Open Court, 1970 (reprint).

BURGER, E. *Spirit Theater.* New York: Kaufman and Greenberg, 1986.

CARRINGTON, H. *The Physical Phenomena of Spiritualism.* London: Chatto and Windus, 1907.

CORDINDA, T. *Thirteen Steps to Mentalism.* Biddeford: The Supreme Magic Company, 1968.

FITZKEE, D. *Magic by Misdirection.* San Rafael, Calif.: San Rafael House, 1945.

———. *The Trick Brain.* San Rafael, Calif.: San Rafael House, 1944.

FULLER, U. *Confessions of a Psychic.* Teaneck, N.J.: Karl Fulves, 1975.

———. *Further Confessions of a Psychic.* Teaneck, N.J.: Karl Fulves, 1980.

HARRIS, B. *Gellerism Revealed.* Calgary: Hades Intemational, 1985.

HYMAN, R. "Cold Reading. How to Convince Strangers That You Know All About Them." *The Zetetic,* 1(2), 1977, 18–37.

KAYE, M. *The Handbook of Mental Magic.* New York: Stein and Day, 1975.

KEENE, M. L. *The Psychic Mafia.* St Martin's Press, 1976.

MCGILL, O. *How to Produce Miracles.* New York. NY: New American Library, Signet Books, 1977.

PAGE, P. *The Big Book of Magic.* London: Sphere Books Ltd, 1977.

PRICE, H. and E. DINGWALL. *Revelations of a Spirit Medium.* London: Kegan Paul, 1922.

WATERS, T. A. *The Encyclopedia of Magic and Magicians.* New York: Facts On File Publications, 1988.

WHALEY, B. *Encyclopedic Dictionary of Magic.* Oakland, Calif.: Jeff Busby Magic Inc, 1989.

WILSON, M. *Mark Wilson's Complete Course in Magic.* Pennsylvania: Courage Books, 1988.

Suppliers

Much of the conjuring and pseudopsychic literature mentioned in this section can be obtained from the following specialist book dealers:

Davenports, 7 Charing Cross, Underground Shopping Arcade, The Strand, London, WC2N 4HZ, UK.

Jeff Busby Magic Inc., 10329 MacArthur Boulevard, Suites 5 and 6, Oakland, CA 94605-5147, USA.

Lee Jacobs Publications, P.O. Box 362-LI75, Pomeroy, Ohio. 45769-0362, USA.

Magic Books by Post, 29 Hill Avenue, Bedminster, Bristol, BS3 4SN, Britain.

Literature concerned with overcoming standard security systems can be obtained from the following specialist book dealers:

Soldier of Fortune, Unit 3a and 3b, Brymau Estate, River Lane, Saltney, Chester, CH4 8RQ, UK.

Loompanics Unlimited, P.O. Box 1197, Port Townsend, WA 98368, USA.

Journals

CONJURING AND PSEUDOPSYCHIC

GENII, The International Conjurors' Magazine. P.O. Box 36068, Los Angeles, CA 90036, USA.

Abracadabra. Goodlife Publications Ltd, 150 New Road, Bromsgrove, Worcestershire, B60 2LG, England.

Magic: The Independent Magicazine for Magicians. 7380 South Eastern Avenue, Suite 124–179, Las Vegas, NV 99123, USA.

Magigram. The Supreme Magic Co. Ltd, 64 High Street, Bideford, Devon, England.

PARAPSYCHOLOGY JOURNALS

European Journal of Parapsychology (1975–). Department of Psychology, University of Edinburgh, 7 George Square, Edinburgh, EH8 9JZ, UK.

Journal of the American Society for Psychical Research. (1907–). American Society for Psychical Research, 5 West 73rd Street, New York, NY 10023, USA.

Journal of Parapsychology (1937–). 402 North Buchanan Boulevard, Durham, NC 27701, USA.

Journal of the Society for Psychical Research (1882-). Society for Psychical Research, 49 Marloes Road, London, W8 6LA, UK.

The Skeptical Inquirer. Box 703, Buffalo, NY 14226-0703, USA.

The Skeptic. P.O. Box 475, Manchester, M60 2TH, UK.

RELATED AREAS

Fortean Times: The Journal of Strange Phenomena. 20 Paul Street, Frome, Somerset, BA11 1DX, UK.

HOAX!, 64 Beechgrove, Aberhonddu, Powys, Cymru, LD3 9ET, UK

Additional Publications of Interest

Cox, W. E. "Guest Editorial: Whether Today's Psi Sensitives?" *The Journal of the American Society for Psychical Research* 87(2), 125–32, 1993.

Fox, J. A. and J. Levin. *How to Work with the Media.* Survival Skills for Scholars series. Volume 2. London: Sage Publications, 1992.

Locke, L. F., W. W. Spirduso, and S. J. Silverman. *Proposals that Work: A Guide for Planning Dissertations and Grant Proposals.* London: Sage Publications, 1993.

Appendix B

Useful Addresses

Conjuring and Pseudopsychic Organizations

BRITAIN

The Magic Circle, The Honorary Secretary, c/o The Victory Services Club, 63/79 Seymour Street, London, W2 2HF, England. Produces a monthly magazine (*The Magic Circular*) for members.

The British Ring of the International Brotherhood of Magicians, H.J. Atkins (Honorary Secretary), Kings Gam, Fritham Court, Fritham, Lyndhurst, Hants., SO43 7HH. Produces a monthly magazine (*The Budget*) for members only.

In addition, a list of many local magic clubs can be found in the weekly magical magazine *Abracadabra* (see Appendix A).

USA

The International Brotherhood of Magicians, Headquarters Office, 103 North Main Street, Bluffton, OH 45817-0089, USA. Produces a monthly magazine (*The Linking Ring*) for members only. This magazine also contains reports from many of the IBM rings both within, and outside of, the USA.

The Society of American Magicians, John Apperson, S.A.M. Membership Development, 2812 Idaho, Granite City, IL 62040, USA. Produces a monthly magazine (*MUM*) for members only.

The Magic Castle, 7001 Franklin Avenue, Hollywood, CA 90028, USA.

Parapsychology Organizations

American Society for Psychical Research, 5 West 73rd Street, New York, NY, 10023, USA.

Rhine Research Center Institute for Parapsychology, 402 North Buchanan Boulevard, Durham, NC 27701, USA.

Koestler Chair of Parapsychology, Psychology Department, Edinburgh University, 7 George Square, Edinburgh, EH8 9JZ, UK.

Society for Psychical Research, 49 Marloes Road, London, W8 6LA, UK.

Parapsychological Association, P.O. Box 12236, Research Triangle Park, NC 27709, USA.

Parapsychology Foundation, 228 East 71st Street, New York, NY 10021, USA.

Parapsychological Sources of Information Center, 2 Plane Tree Lane, Dix Hills, NY 11746, USA.

The Committee for the Scientific Investigation of Claims of the Paranormal (CSICOP), Box 703, Buffalo, NY 14226-0703, USA.

Appendix C

Useful Security Products

This appendix briefly outlines some of the commercially available security products that may be of use to researchers testing psychic claimants.

Securing Valuable Material

Researchers may wish to store certain material (e.g., targets, experimental protocols, results, etc.) in a highly secure area. If they are able to devote an entire room to this purpose it could be made secure in several different ways. High-security alarm systems, doors, and locks could be fitted to the room. However, such products are relatively expensive, and researchers may be more concerned with a pseudopsychic entering the room undetected, as opposed to using easily detectable force to break into it. If this is the case, researchers could employ "tamper-evident" products to render the room secure. Many companies supply tamper-evident plastic seals or stickers. When in place (e.g., around the handles of a double door) they cannot be removed without showing signs of interference. In addition, they carry a unique security number and so cannot be removed and replaced with a duplicate seal or sticker.

When securing a room with this type of product researchers should ensure that there are no additional ways in which the room could be secretly entered. For example, a pseudopsychic may attempt to remove the pins that hold the door hinges together, so that the door would open on the hinge side. Researchers should obviously ensure that any additional entrance points into the room (e.g., the windows, ceiling panels) are as well protected as the doors themselves.

When wishing to make secure a relatively small amount of material, researchers may find it inconvenient to protect a whole room. Instead, they may prefer to house the material in a cabinet. High-security cabinets can be purchased for exactly this purpose. Alternatively, a normal cabinet could be converted into a highly secure container by using the tamper-evident products described above.

Finally, researchers may wish to render secure a relatively small item, and may be unable, or unwilling, to go to the trouble of constructing a secure cabinet simply for this purpose. For example, a claimant may wish to take target material away from the laboratory, and work with it in his or her own home. Some small items (eg., target pictures in an ESP study) could be protected by tamper-evident bags. These bags are usually constructed from polyethylene, and cannot be slit and resealed without detection.

The bags are sealed by means of a self-adhesive strip that runs along the top of the bag. This strip reveals signs of physical tampering, including attempts to peel off the strip, the application of heat or cold, and the use of various solvents. In addition, to prevent the envelope being opened and then replaced by a duplicate bag, each individual envelope carries a unique identification number. Delanov, Morris, Watt, and Wiseman (1993) describe an ESP study using exactly this procedure. When running some PK experiments, researchers may wish to protect a take-home target in a small box, as opposed to a bag. If this were the case, researchers could employ the "strong" boxes that are commercially produced for guarding valuables in transit. Alternatively, a normal box could be made more secure by sealing it with some of the tamper-evident seals and stickers discussed above.

Covert Observation

Researchers may wish to engage in the covert observation of a claimant. For example, claimants may state that they are more comfortable if researchers leave the experimental room while they attempt to be psychic. If this were the case, researchers could covertly observe claimants by using a simple, and unobtrusive, closed circuit television system. The cameras used within many of these systems are only a few inches in size and thus could be easily installed in a room without raising the claimant's suspicion. During field investigations researchers may wish to secretly videotape the claimant. This could be achieved by employing a miniature self-contained video camera, perhaps built into an innocent-looking object such as a briefcase. Again, such products are commercially available. Finally, researchers may also be interested to know that some companies produce "night sights," which can be used to observe, and film, in conditions of near darkness.

Electronic Countersurveillance

Researchers may wish to detect pseudopsychics who are using electronic transmitting/receiving devices to fake telepathic ability. In addition, researchers may wish to discover whether a pseudopsychic has placed a "bug" on the researchers themselves, or in their office(s), and is thus able to gain information that will help them fabricate psi (e.g., the nature of a target, the controls which will be used in a forthcoming study, etc.). If researchers are concerned that such devices are, or may be, in operation, their presence can be detected by use of commercially available countersurveillance apparatus.

Searching a Claimant

When running some studies researchers may wish to search a claimant. Such searches may be designed to discover whether the claimant is carrying any apparatus that may help fake psychic ability, or any small objects that he or she will later claim to have made appear during the experiment. Many companies specialize in short training courses designed to teach individuals how to perform quick and effective searches. In addition, researchers could employ any of the handheld metal detectors to discover whether the claimant is concealing any metal objects on or within his body.